Planning and Environment Linkages Program

A Guide to Measuring Progress
in Linking Transportation
Planning and Environmental
Analysis

December 2009

Prepared for:
Office of Planning and
Office of Project Development and Environmental Review
Federal Highway Administration
U.S. Department of Transportation

Prepared by:
John A. Volpe National Transportation Systems Center
Research and Innovative Technology Administration
U.S. Department of Transportation

Acknowledgements

This U.S. Department of Transportation (USDOT) Federal Highway Administration (FHWA) report was prepared with assistance from the USDOT John A. Volpe National Transportation Systems Center (Volpe Center). The project team included Michael Culp of FHWA's Office of Project Development and Environmental Review; Sharlene Reed of FHWA's Office of Planning; Anna Biton, Gina Barberio, and Rachael Barolsky of the Volpe Center's Transportation Policy, Planning and Organizational Excellence Division; and Gina Filosa of Cambridge Systematics.

The project team wishes to thank the numerous individuals from State DOTs, MPOs, and resource agencies who graciously offered their time, knowledge, and assistance in the development of this report.

This research has been funded by the FHWA's Office of Planning, Environment and Realty's Surface Transportation Environment and Planning Cooperative Research Program (STEP).

Table of Contents

A Guide to Measuring Progress in Linking Transportation Planning and Environmental Analysis

Transportation agencies use a variety of metrics to document progress toward achieving specific goals and objectives. This guide, developed by Federal Highway Administration's (FHWA) Planning and Environmental Linkages (PEL) program, is intended to help State Departments of Transportation (DOTs), metropolitan planning organizations (MPOs), and local transportation agencies develop individual programs to measure success toward linking transportation planning and environmental analysis. This guide provides a framework for establishing measures that transportation agencies can utilize to develop their own measurement programs. To illustrate implementation of the framework, it provides an overall goal of linking transportation planning and environmental analysis, four sample objectives, and an array of example metrics to track progress toward achieving these goals and objectives.

Overview of Linking Transportation Planning and Environmental Analysis

Linking transportation planning and environmental analysis requires an integrated and collaborative approach to transportation decisionmaking. Such an approach promotes the consideration of environmental, community, and economic goals early in the transportation planning process, and supports carrying those considerations through project development, design, construction, and maintenance. Figure 1 depicts some of the activities and people that can support the incorporation of environmental considerations throughout the transportation decisionmaking process

Figure 1: Integrated approach to transportation decisionmaking

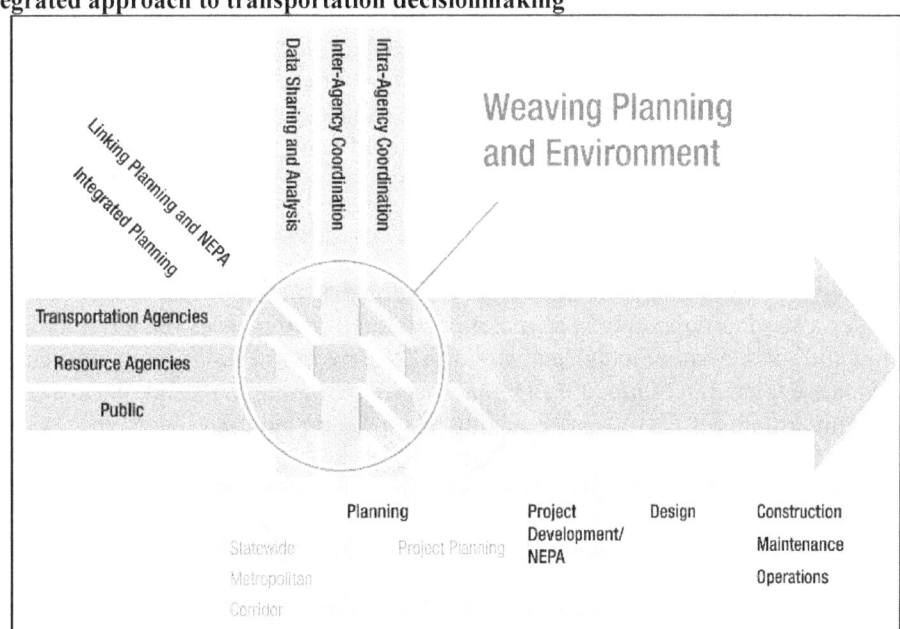

An integrated approach to transportation planning also recognizes the continuing need to link short and long-range transportation planning and corridor level planning conducted by State and local governments to the planning processes performed by environmental protection, historic preservation, resource conservation, and land use management agencies. Such an approach to transportation planning enables planners and the public to consider the costs and benefits of decisions in a comprehensive manner. This provides the opportunity to address complex social, economic and environmental challenges early in the planning process, as well as avoid and minimize impacts on natural and human resources.

These linkages also support the unification of the transportation planning process with the National Environmental Policy Act (NEPA) environmental review process. Such an approach encourages that the data and analysis used to prepare transportation plans and the subsequent results of the planning process feed into the NEPA process. Incorporating and relying on planning products to support NEPA analysis and documentation creates a cohesive flow between the two processes, and minimizes the duplication of work and resulting delays in project development. Similarly, the NEPA process should establish a feedback loop to provide baseline information developed for individual projects to assist the planning process in identifying potential additional long and short range impacts of transportation programs and projects.

Why this Guide is Needed

The use of performance-based measures by transportation agencies is a growing trend that is expected to continue. While most of the traditional measures used by transportation agencies focus on system conditions or operations (such as accessibility, mobility, safety, and operational efficiency), there has been little application to tracking the successes of integrated planning and environmental stewardship efforts. Such successes can be difficult to quantify and measure, as they often relate to planning process changes and coordination efforts whose results may not be immediately obvious.

Establishing metrics related to integrated planning and environmental stewardship will allow transportation agencies to demonstrate to the public, internal leadership, and external partners – including resource and regulatory agencies – that they are committed to monitoring their progress in integrating environmental considerations throughout the transportation decisionmaking process. Metrics will help agencies that are taking steps to integrate transportation planning and environmental analysis to determine whether those activities are meeting their intended objectives. Metrics will also help agencies utilize impartial data to identify challenges or obstacles to achieving the identified goals, and identify potential needs for changes in policy or implementation approach.

Framework for Measuring Progress

This guide provides a starting point to help agencies create their own metrics related to progress in linking transportation planning and environmental analysis. The framework for developing metrics includes four primary tasks that are depicted in Figure 2: 1) Define specific program goals and objectives; 2) Develop a set of metrics to demonstrate results towards reaching the defined goals and objectives; 3) Assess baseline and develop targets; and 4) Measure and report results.

Figure 2: Suggested framework for creating measures

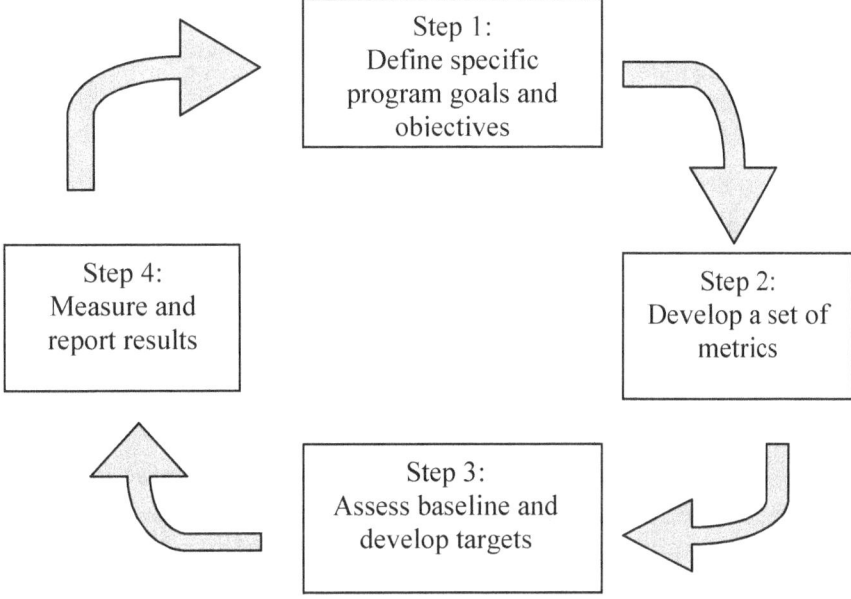

Step 1: Define program goals and objectives

The primary purpose of a metric is to track progress toward defined goals and objectives. To begin, an agency needs to determine its overall goal for linking transportation planning and environmental analysis, and outline objectives related to the attainment of the goal. A goal is a general statement of what the program hopes to accomplish. An objective is a specific, measurable condition that must be attained in order to accomplish the program goal.

Effective measuring requires clearly defined goals and objectives that cover the breadth of the transportation program or activities. If the objectives provide only partial coverage of the related program, it is likely that monitoring will likewise be incomplete in its reporting of important impacts.

In order to illustrate how the framework outlined in Figure 2 can be applied to measuring successes in linking transportation planning and environmental analysis, this guidebook identifies an overall goal for linking transportation planning and environmental analysis, as well as four sample objectives to achieve the goal. The sample objectives included in the guide are intended as a starting point to help transportation agencies define their own agency-specific objectives. Each agency will need to determine the appropriate objectives to meet its particular planning and project development processes and needs.

The program objectives included in this guide are supported by various implementation activities that are discussed in detail throughout. Setting targets for the outcomes of various implementation activities is discussed in Step 3.

Goal: Create a seamless transportation decisionmaking process that minimizes duplication of effort, promotes environmental stewardship, and reduces delay from planning through project implementation

- **Sample Objective 1:** Foster the early and ongoing involvement of regulatory and resource agencies in the planning process.

- **Sample Objective 2:** Incorporate natural and cultural considerations into the transportation planning process and development of the transportation improvement program in order to achieve community goals and avoid adversely impacting priority resources.

- **Sample Objective 3:** Identify preliminary regional environmental mitigation needs as part of the planning process, thereby providing opportunities to develop more effective environmental mitigation measures.

- **Sample Objective 4:** Utilize planning level information and products in NEPA analysis and documentation to improve decision-making and streamline project delivery.

An integrated approach to transportation planning requires coordination between the transportation planning and environmental review departments, as well as coordination among transportation, land-use and resource agencies. Because multiple stakeholders will play a role in achieving the goals and objectives, it is essential that they are developed through a cooperative effort among all stakeholders.

Step 2: Develop a set of metrics to demonstrate results toward reaching the defined goals and objectives

Once an agency has established its goals and objectives, the next step is to develop metrics to measure its progress toward attaining those objectives. Agencies can use a mix of output and outcome measures to gauge their progress toward linking transportation planning and environmental analysis.

Output measures track the products delivered or activities performed by a program or agency. *Outcome measures* reflect the intended result(s) or impact(s) of the outputs on the agency's goals or objectives.

Output measures are typically easier to monitor and are often under more direct control of agency actions, whereas outcome measures are typically broader and more likely to be affected by the actions of others. Because many aspects of linking transportation planning and the environmental analysis are outside the direct control of a transportation agency, it is important to utilize various types of measures related to both outputs and outcomes. In situations where the final results are beyond the single control of the transportation agency, the agency can use the output measures to at least evaluate its own processes and actions toward achieving the broader goals.

The following characteristics should be considered when selecting measures:

- **Valid** – there is an explicit link between the measures and the program goals and objectives.

- **Understandable** – the measures are clearly defined and easily interpreted by those using the information.

- **Objective** – the measures are based on objective and observable information.

- **Available** – the measures are based on the availability of robust data and supporting analysis methods. The information is available and can be used to inform current decisionmaking.

- **Cost Effective** – the cost of collecting the required data is reasonable.

- **Concise** – the number of measures are limited to those that are most significant to measure the success of the program/activity.

- **Controllable** – measures that the agency cannot influence by agency action or policy should not be included, or should be developed in concert with agencies that share an influence over the measure.

Since one measure will not satisfy all desired criteria, a mix of measures is needed. Each measure must satisfy different criteria and be appropriate for different purposes.

It is important to note that measuring progress and successes toward linking transportation planning and environmental analysis differs from the typical performance measurement traditionally used by transportation agencies, such as those related to system operations. For example, linking transportation planning and environmental process activities may focus more on building relationships between agencies or incorporating diverse data sets, the outcomes of which may not be immediately obvious. Effective measuring requires a combination of both quantitative and qualitative indicators, in order to account for the impacts of coordination and process improvements.

This guide includes suggested metrics for both output and outcome measures, as well as a mix of quantitative and qualitative measures, for each of the four sample objectives. As depicted in Figure 3 the measures link directly to the objectives and overarching goal. The output measures are tied directly to the activities an agency implements in order to achieve its objective (e.g. the number of staff trained). The outcome measures relate to the results that those implementation activities are intended to achieve (e.g. increased knowledge of the planning process).

It is important to note that the examples included in this guide do not represent an exhaustive list of appropriate applicable measures. Furthermore, not all of the measures featured will be relevant to all agencies or to all contexts (e.g., metropolitan, statewide, long-range, or corridor planning, transportation improvement program (TIP) development, or project development). As agencies develop their specific goals and objectives for linking transportation planning and environmental analysis, they are encouraged to use the samples provided in this guide as a base from which to refine and expand upon to meet their own needs.

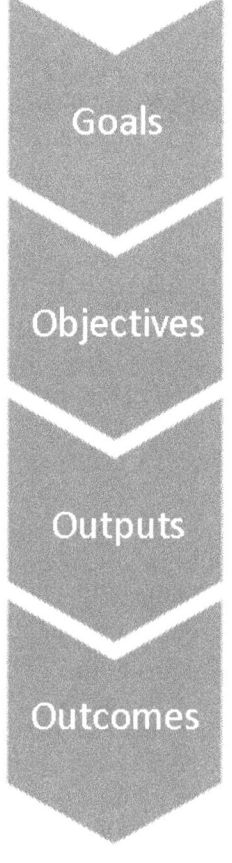

Figure 3: Each output and outcome measure has an explicit link to the objective.

Step 3: Assess baseline and develop targets

Targets create a vision for what an agency would like to achieve in the future, and are used to evaluate results achieved compared to the results desired. Targets are essential to measuring success, as they provide the context and the meaning to a measure. For example, simply measuring the number or percentage of projects meeting certain criteria is not meaningful in itself. An agency must first determine the target number or percentage of projects that they hope to achieve. An agency should create realistic targets that are based on planned actions.

There are a variety of ways to set targets. One option is for targets to be time bound (e.g., conduct X number of trainings by Y time). Another option is to base targets on a specific percentage achieved (e.g., increase participation in interagency meetings by X percentage).

In order to measure progress and success in meeting its targets, an agency must understand its baseline condition. From this assessment of current conditions compared with desired end results, the agency can develop a plan of action and track progress over time. The baseline condition can be determined in a variety of ways, including using historically collected data and conducting baseline surveys.

Because appropriate targets depend so much on context and agency needs and priorities, this guide does not provide example targets. Instead, the guide provides tips and suggestions for agencies to consider when developing targets associated with each of the outlined objectives. The measures suggested in this guide are also intended to be customized based on an agency's specific targets. As a result, the measures are general enough that they can be tailored to meet the targets and needs of the agency. For example, where a measure may suggest using a number or percentage, it is the agency's responsibility to first determine the desired number or percentage to use as its target.

Step 4: Measure and report results

Once an agency defines its targets, it must identify the data to collect to evaluate results for comparison to the target. Agencies should examine the types of data currently collected internally, as well as the data collected by partner agencies, to avoid duplicating data collection efforts. It is unlikely that all of the data needed to evaluate results will be available. In such instances, an agency can prioritize its data needs, and over time can begin collecting the relevant information.

Agencies should measure progress throughout the transportation planning and project development process, and use the results to facilitate internal communication and discussion about what is currently working and where improvements are needed. The data collected as part of the measurement program are not meant to single out any individual in the agency. Quite the contrary – the data provide a framework for an impartial and constructive decision-making process aimed at improving the agency's program. The data can be used to help identify work programs or resource allocations that need to be adjusted, and to determine the appropriate policy or implementation activities to address those needs.

For example, an agency may decide to conduct staff trainings in order to increase staff's knowledge in a given topic. The agency sets as a target a percentage of staff to train over the next year. This number can then be tracked as an *output* measure. The corresponding *outcome* measure could be that staff demonstrate a greater understanding in that topic area. At the end of the reporting period, the agency could review the results and decide that the trainings have been effective at achieving the desired outcome and therefore the target should remain the same. Conversely, the agency may determine that despite meeting its target for the number of staff members trained, the outcomes are not improving and, therefore, it should increase its training target for the coming period, or perhaps it is time to consider an alternate approach to achieving the intended outcome. In either case, the output measure provides an impartial value that can be used to evaluate an agency's progress in meeting its own objectives and assessing the best approach for planning future activities.

How to Use this Guide

This guide is intended to assist transportation agencies in determining how to evaluate progress and success toward linking transportation planning and environmental analysis. The remainder of this guide is organized around the four sample objectives that were highlighted earlier. Each section can be used on its own or in conjunction with the other sections. It should be noted that State DOTs and MPOs are not required to adopt or use any of the goals, objectives, and measures listed in this guide. This guide provides suggestions and tools as a resource to agencies that are interested in exploring and initiating performance measurement of their linkage activities, but it does not make judgments about the effectiveness of any of the individual activities.

Each section is structured under the following subheadings:

- *Purpose of the objective* – provides information on the specific objective, discussing its importance, general tips for implementation, and key implementation challenges.

- _Tips for developing strategies and setting targets_ – suggests several actions and issues to consider for implementation that will help in setting agency-specific targets, and therefore assist in measurement. Many of these tips highlight the importance of setting appropriate targets (i.e. identifying the _right_ information, data, people on a team, etc.), before measuring the number achieved. This provides an important reminder to ensure that the activities and corresponding measures will supply the best information about meeting program goals. As discussed above, this guide will not propose specific targets for an agency, but does pose some of the important questions and issues that an agency should consider in setting targets.

- _Example measures_ – provides tables with sample output and outcome measures relevant to each objective and the tips. Note that none of the measures include a target number or percentage for comparison; this is the responsibility of the user to provide. The tables include suggested data sources and ways to use the data to measure both the outputs and outcomes. The tables also reference examples of State DOTs and MPOs utilizing the measure as part of their own tracking programs. The references discuss where and how the highlighted agencies collect and report the information.

Sample Objective 1

Foster the early and continuous involvement of regulatory and resource agencies in the transportation planning process.

Purpose

While natural and historic resource agencies are intricately involved with transportation project development and environmental review processes, historically they have had limited participation in transportation planning. Current transportation planning regulations, however, require transportation agencies to consult with resource agencies during the development of long-range plans (see 23 CFR 450).

Involving resource agencies early and on a continuous basis during the transportation planning process has the potential to enhance the protection of natural and cultural resources and streamline the project development process. Collaboration among experts in transportation and conservation agencies is essential to effectively utilize available data and tools. By obtaining input from resource and regulatory agencies early in the planning process, transportation planners can better identify potential environmental concerns before detailed project development begins. This will avoid and minimize impacts on natural resources and enables effective environmental stewardship. In addition, facilitating interagency participation and coordination early in the planning process can reduce the potential for conflict and minimize delays that result when environmental issues are not uncovered prior to project implementation.

While the benefits of early involvement abound, resource and transportation agencies face challenges in fulfilling this objective. Involving regulatory and resource agencies in the transportation planning process may require a significant change in the way these organizations currently interact with transportation agencies. While such agencies are familiar with the project development and environmental review processes, many lack the necessary knowledge of the transportation planning process that precedes this work. Furthermore, providing input into transportation planning will often require more staff time during the planning stages; however, numerous demands on resource agency staff limit their ability to participate in activities beyond fulfilling their procedural responsibilities. Finally, resource agencies do not have reciprocal consultation requirements for transportation planning. Transportation agencies should recognize these challenges and identify ways to support stakeholder involvement throughout the process.

Tips for Developing Strategies and Setting Targets

Transportation agencies should consider the following key elements when developing strategies that will include statewide partners in transportation decisionmaking.

Identify appropriate stakeholders – Identify which regulatory, and resource agencies to involve in the transportation planning process. In order to facilitate interagency coordination, agencies may choose to form an interagency working group. When such a group is formed, it is important to ensure that those involved represent a proper mix of expertise, including natural, cultural, and historic resource agencies at the Federal, Tribal, State, regional, and local levels. It is also important to include staff that have both the necessary technical knowledge of the key issues as well as the authority to make decisions for their agency.

It may be effective to invite certain non-governmental organizations (NGOs) to be involved with the process as well, as they sometimes have the most detailed information about conservation needs in the region or particular resources. This option is worth exploring, but should be considered carefully, so as not to appear to show a bias toward one organization or another. Expectations for involvement in the process should be made clear from the beginning.

Determine effective communication techniques – Develop a robust outreach plan to engage regulatory and resource agencies in the transportation planning process. Written invitations requesting participation can often be overlooked. In contrast, personal and direct communication, such as a telephone call or meeting, provides for more meaningful interaction between the stakeholders and improves the likelihood that resource and regulatory agencies will participate in the planning process.

Determine and communicate desired level of involvement from stakeholder agencies in transportation planning process – Develop a shared vision of how agencies will be involved in the transportation decisionmaking process in order to set a standard for measuring interagency coordination. This includes identifying the appropriate times during transportation planning when environmental, regulatory, and resource agencies will be included, as well as identifying effective communication mechanisms for various agencies. Creating formal interagency agreements, such as Memoranda of Understanding (MOUs) and Memoranda of Agreement (MOAs) can help agencies to define roles and responsibilities. A formal agreement can also help to identify specific benchmarks in the transportation decisionmaking process when resource and regulatory agency participation is most needed. It is essential that stakeholders be present and involved in developing these benchmarks.

It is equally as important to explain to stakeholders early-on the intent to use planning level information as the foundation for when the project development/NEPA process begins. Understanding how their involvement in planning can impact project outcomes will provide additional incentives for resource and regulatory agencies to participate in the transportation planning process.

Determine level of understanding of agency planning processes – Each agency is familiar with its own planning process, but may not be familiar with the types of data and planning products produced by other agencies. Effective collaboration among resource and transportation agencies requires that each understand the other's language, processes, and goals. In order to enhance understanding, agencies can conduct cross-trainings or host interagency forums. Creating a flow chart of the timelines for decision-making and the associated parties involved for each planning process may be helpful.

Determine funding and staffing needs – Determine the level of funding and staff time needed to ensure meaningful involvement in transportation planning. Numerous demands on resource agency staff will limit their ability to participate in transportation planning. If insufficient staff or financial resources present a barrier to participation in transportation planning, transportation agencies may consider using Federal-aid project funds to support transportation planning activities, including dedicated staffing at resource and regulatory agencies (see 23 U.S.C 139(j)).

Example Measures

Establishing metrics can help agencies understand the extent to which alternative activities are successfully leading to the increased involvement of environmental agencies in the transportation planning process. The following table provides examples of output and outcome measures that an agency can use to track its progress toward meeting the objective, as well as possible data sources for the measures. As was discussed earlier in this guide, for each measure an agency would establish targets based on its needs and priorities. The agency would evaluate results achieved compared to the targets it established for itself.

Output Measures	Data Source(s)/ How to Use
Number of agency cross-trainings conducted	Track trainings offered
Number of staff/agencies that participate in training (managers and professionals)	Track attendance at staff trainings
Number of natural, cultural, and historic resource agencies at the Federal, Tribal, State, regional, and local levels involved in an interagency committee	Execution of agency agreements
Number of interagency meetings conducted	Track number of meetings
Participation rate of members in interagency meetings that focus on input to transportation plans	Track attendance at interagency meetings of individuals who are actually involved in the decision-making process or will have continued participation in the process
Number of resource and/or regulatory agencies that have positions dedicated to ensuring coordination with transportation planning	Track funding provided to agencies to support transportation planning activities

Outcome Measures	Data Source(s)/ How to Use
Decrease in the number of major design changes due to environmental factors in project development	Track the number and reason for major design changes [11]
Satisfaction of resource and regulatory agencies with the transportation planning process	Stakeholder surveys [12]
Increase in percentage of stakeholders who felt their input was considered in the development of transportation plans	Stakeholder surveys [13]
Decrease in the number of permit modifications	Track the number and reason for permit modifications
Regulatory and resource agencies demonstrate a greater understanding of the planning processes and products of transportation agencies (and vice versa)	Stakeholder surveys

Examples in Practice

[11] The Massachusetts Highway Department (MassHighway) tracks performance measures related to streamlining project delivery. One of the agency's project delivery performance measures is adherence to a time and budget schedule. As a data source for this measure, MassHighway tracks the causes and frequency of both internal and external construction time extensions, which provides information to identify the most common causes of delays.

[12] The Florida DOT uses annual surveys to assess the Efficient Transportation Decision Making (ETDM) program, a streamlined process for planning transportation projects, conducting environmental reviews,

and developing and permitting projects. The surveys, which are distributed to agencies involved in the ETDM process, are used to assess the performance of the ETDM process itself as well as the performance of the agencies.

[13] To assess customer involvement in transportation decisionmaking, the MoDOT conducts an annual telephone survey of a representative statewide sample of 800 citizens. Each year, customers are asked a variety of questions regarding DOT activities. They are also asked to rate MoDOT on a scale of 1 to 10. By asking the same questions each year, MoDOT is able to track trends. In areas where customers were dissatisfied, improvement needs were identified and targeted.

Sample Objective 2

Incorporate natural and cultural considerations into the transportation planning process and development of the transportation improvement program (TIP) in order to achieve community goals and avoid adversely impacting priority resources.

Purpose

Transportation, land use, and environmental resource planning are typically undertaken separately and by different agencies. This separation makes it difficult to understand the connections among the various systems and how changes in one system may affect another. An integrated approach to transportation planning recognizes that transportation is but one part of a larger system that includes ecological, economic development, and community goals. When agencies develop transportation plans, including long-range, TIP and corridor, with input from other agencies, they are better able to develop programs and projects that meet the goals and objectives that regions set for their social and physical development.

The successful integration of transportation planning with land use, natural, and cultural resource system planning relies upon the sharing of data, information, and expertise among resource and transportation agencies. Information sharing among these agencies helps to ensure that all participants are working from the same basic starting point and can reduce the likelihood that earlier decisions will be reopened once project development activities have begun. It also allows for early preparation to consider comprehensive mitigation needs. While resource considerations can be integrated at any stage of the transportation process, it is best to compare plans and data early in the process since it enables transportation agencies to flag potential problems before narrowing potential alternative transportation solutions. Waiting to identify and address inconsistent or incompatible goals and priorities among transportation and resource agencies is one of the main reasons for conflict and delay in program/project development.

It is important for an agency to develop a system for analyzing natural, social and cultural resource issues during the planning process. Data support tools such as geographic information systems (GIS) provide one way to incorporate environmental information with transportation planning needs. Natural and cultural resource data layers, such as the location of wetlands and rare wildlife habitats, can be overlaid with existing and planned transportation networks to identify areas of potential concern. This analysis, coupled with expert input from resource agencies, provides the opportunity to avoid and minimize impacts on natural resources and enables effective environmental stewardship.

While geospatial data can provide a valuable tool to analyze the resource impacts of transportation plans, obtaining and incorporating such data can pose several challenges. First, transportation agencies may not be aware of the existing and available data (internally and from other agencies). In addition, it can be challenging to obtain accurate, comprehensive, and consistent data sets from other agencies, and maintaining regular updates can be difficult. In contrast, transportation agencies may have a plethora of data, but have difficulty identifying which elements are actually relevant to the task at hand. Because more information is not necessarily better if it does not address the most important issues, it is in the agency's interest to carefully plan how it allocates time and resources to data gathering.

Tips for Developing Strategies and Setting Targets

Transportation agencies should consider the following key elements when developing strategies on how to include environmental considerations early in transportation planning and TIP development.

Identify key land use, natural, and cultural resource issues – Identify and understand the key issues that are most important to consider early in the planning process. To begin, consider natural environmental issues such as wetlands, wildlife, cultural resources, and sensitive habitats, as well as human issues such as access needs, important community centers and attractions, and key travel corridors. To the extent possible, understanding the unique context and history of the planning area will lead to a planning and project development process that better serves the needs of all involved.

Identify data and information sources – Identify the data and information sources that will be necessary to appropriately address key human and natural environmental issues. The planning process involves compilation and analysis of a broad range of environmental, historic, archeological, cultural, and social data. Consider the following questions:

- What transportation and environmental, economic and/or social resource datasets are essential to further clarify the important issues and identify potential issues or solutions? This may be an iterative process as a data review will sometimes uncover issues. Other times, identifying issues leads to the need for additional data.

- What data are already available at your agency, and where else might you be able to obtain additional information? Sources of information that may be relevant include known future development, State/local resource conservation management plans, State wildlife action plans, watershed plans, statewide geographic data clearinghouses, and land use plans. Some of this information may not be immediately available, but can be obtained upon request. Developing stronger relationships with regulatory and resource agencies (as described in Objective 1) can provide a venue for identifying appropriate data and sources.

- Are any special agreements necessary to use and display the data? Some data are sensitive and not publicly shared, particularly data that are related to certain historic resources. Identify how data can be shared while protecting the confidentiality of sensitive data.

- How can you present the data so that it clearly conveys the relationships between the transportation system and natural resources? GIS mapping can be particularly effective in displaying such information.

- Are you able to identify gaps in existing data sources? For example, a lack of data on a particular area may indicate that there are no significant issues to be concerned with, or it might mean that the area has not yet been surveyed. When accepting data from other sources, be sure to ask about and record any information on gaps or inconsistencies in the data. Identify and note any such gaps in the data that are collected internally.

Consider transportation system flexibility – Consider existing and future flexibility in project identification and selection. A project that seems to meet some needs related to capacity or access may present other concerns to the community or sensitive resources. Consider the following questions:

- What flexibility is there for design/alignment alternatives for new or expanded facilities? During the planning process, explore whether an alternate route or design, or a policy decision could accomplish some of the same goals without compromising environmental and community resources.

- Are there opportunities for mitigation banking? What kind of preservation is necessary for those areas? (See objective three for more in depth information on mitigation.)

Develop criteria for project selection and prioritization – Consider developing formal conservation and environmental criteria to use when selecting and prioritizing projects during the planning and TIP processes. Using defined criteria to prioritize projects can assist agencies in identifying and addressing environmental concerns, as well as systematically evaluating necessary trade-offs associated with project-related decisions. It might be useful to utilize GIS in screening or evaluating the projects based on the criteria in order to better understand issues and potential impacts.

Consider ability to screen unreasonable alternatives – Information and data collected during the planning process can be used to determine the appropriate range of alternatives to evaluate during the NEPA process. During the planning process, it may be possible to narrow some alternatives based on the environmental data analysis and project evaluation screening. In this case, it is very important to thoroughly document the decisions and reasons to ensure they can be passed along to the NEPA process and key evaluations are not duplicated. Alternatives that were subjected to agency and public review and subsequently determined to be infeasible can be omitted from the detailed analysis of alternatives in the NEPA document, as long as the rationale for elimination is explained in the NEPA document.

Example Measures

Establishing metrics can help agencies understand the extent to which important environmental considerations are incorporated into the transportation planning and project development process. The following table provides examples of output and outcome measures that an agency can use to track its progress toward meeting the objective. As was discussed earlier in this guide, for each measure an agency would establish targets based on its needs and priorities. The agency would evaluate results achieved compared to the targets it established for itself.

Output Measures	Data Source(s)/ How to Use
Agency has clearly articulated and published environmental policy and/or conservation strategies from which to base future decisions	Compare policy and/or strategies with current implementation practices
Relevant data layers are identified, obtained, and used in analysis (and reliability/accuracy is known and documented)	Count/calculate the number/percentage of data layers identified as relevant that have been obtained and used as compared to the target.
Relevant environmentally-sensitive areas identified and mapped	Count the number/percent of environmentally-sensitive areas that have been mapped as compared to the target
Transportation network miles with current resource maps	Identify the percentage of available resource mapping and compare to transportation network[21]
Social/economic/environmental criteria used in project selection and prioritization	Presence of criteria, which are used in decisionmaking
Proposed projects achieving a target score on the environmental/priority screening	Tally scores of evaluated projects to identify the number of projects the meet the target score[22]
Projects that either avoid or minimize impacts	Identify project activity in the vicinity of a known threatened or endangered species or critical habitat[23]

Outcome Measures	Data Source(s)/ How to Use
High priority environmental habitats and connections between them are protected (e.g. acreage of land preserved; number or type of species protected)	GIS data; Discussions with resource experts at appropriate agencies
Improvement to species, habitats, and wetlands	Use indicators such as: • acres of habitat restored versus acres of habitat affected[24] • acres of wetlands restored • acres of land preserved based on final recommended network versus other alternatives[25]

Examples in Practice

[21] The Oregon Collaborative Environmental and Transportation Agreement for Streamlining (CETAS) Work Plan for 2006-2008 included an element for all participating agencies on the CETAS Team to provide support in merging natural and cultural resource data, including GIS and GPS, into a single cohesive, accessible database. This high-priority database will provide integrated natural and cultural resource spatial data relevant to transportation-related decisionmaking.

[22] To recognize transportation project designs that incorporate a high level of environmental sustainability, New York State DOT (NYSDOT) is implementing "GreenLITES (Leadership In Transportation and Environmental Sustainability)," a project rating program. GreenLITES is a self-certification program that distinguishes transportation projects and operations based on the extent to which they incorporate sustainable choices. This is primarily an internal management program for NYSDOT to measure its performance, recognize good practices, and identify where it needs to improve. The program also provides the agency with a way to demonstrate to the public how it is advancing sustainable practices. NYSDOT project designs and operations are evaluated for sustainable practices and, based on the total credits received, an appropriate certification level is assigned. The rating system recognizes varying certification levels, with the highest level going to designs and operational groups that clearly advance the state of sustainable transportation solutions.

[23] The Missouri DOT (MoDOT) tracks projects that have identified activity in the vicinity of a known threatened or endangered species or critical habitat. This information, which is updated quarterly, does not include most MoDOT projects, as it only counts projects that protect or restore sensitive habitats that could not be avoided. This measure does not count projects that avoid sensitive habitats.

[24] To identify whether natural and cultural resources were enhanced, left whole, or reduced, the New Mexico State Highway Transportation Department's engineering and environmental staff evaluate each project for which an EIS, EA, or complex categorical exclusion is prepared. A ranking is applied based on a scale of 1 to 3.

[25] The Virginia Department of Transportation (VDOT) is committed to creating better connections between land use and transportation planning. As a measure of performance, VDOT tracks trends on the acreage of land preserved statewide.

Sample Objective 3

Identify preliminary regional environmental mitigation needs as part of the planning process, thereby providing opportunities to develop more effective environmental mitigation measures.

Purpose

The goals of transportation and environmental agencies can conflict when the transportation planning process identifies transportation system needs that would build in or near potentially sensitive areas. Traditionally, most mitigation has been based at the project level; however, the transportation planning regulations (23 CFR 450) extend the mitigation requirement into planning. By considering the cumulative impacts of the proposed transportation system during the planning process, agencies can consider mitigation activities on a broader scale than individual projects may allow. This offers agencies the opportunity to identify activities that have the greatest potential to protect, restore, and enhance the environmental factors affected by the plan.

The Council on Environmental Quality (CEQ) regulations (40 CFR 1508.20) defines mitigation as:

- Avoiding the impact altogether by not taking a certain action or parts of an action.
- Minimizing impacts by limiting the degree or magnitude of the action and its implementation.
- Rectifying the impact by repairing, rehabilitating, or restoring the affected environment.
- Reducing or eliminating the impact over time by preservation and maintenance operations during the life of the action.
- Compensating for the impact by replacing or providing substitute resources or environments.

Incorporating environmental considerations into the transportation planning process through data analysis or interagency coordination enables agencies to identify potential sites for mitigation activities. In some instances, however, the agency leading the planning process, such as an MPO, is rarely involved in project development, where the mitigation projects are implemented. Therefore, coordination between planning agencies and those in charge of executing projects is critical to ensure that agencies understand their roles in defining and implementing effective mitigation.

Tips for Developing Strategies and Setting Targets

When developing regional mitigation strategies, transportation agencies should:

Identify appropriate data and information sources – Identify the data and information sources that are necessary to appropriately identify priority habitats, potential areas of concern, and potential conservation sites. Sources of information that may be relevant include conservation maps, cultural and historic inventories, wildlife action plans, land use plans, and watershed plans.

Seek resource agency participation in identifying potential environmental impacts and mitigation options – Consider which agencies and staff are most appropriate to participate in mitigation discussions. For example, invite agencies that regulate priority resources in the study area and staff who are knowledgeable about the study area. Conduct regular meetings or form an interagency workgroup to analyze data and discuss options. Be sure that the different agencies have a consistent understanding of general mitigation definitions and needs. Also consider how each agency conducts its own planning process, and try to coordinate activities to improve process efficiency and effectiveness.

Consider coordination needs between MPO/Regional Planning Organizations and state-level activities – MPOs focus on long-range planning, while other agencies implement the plans on a project level. It is critical that the discussions and analyses regarding mitigation are provided to implementing agencies through plans and background materials. If this information is not provided to agencies, they risk losing the foundation that was built during the planning process. State DOTs can help bring resource agency contacts into discussions with MPOs. In addition, State DOTs or statewide data clearinghouses have access to a wealth of data and GIS resources.

Consider opportunities for multi-project mitigation – Multi-project mitigation involves using a single, typically large, off-site mitigation effort to serve as compensation for impacts resulting from multiple transportation projects.[a] This form of mitigation can offer unique opportunities to more effectively consolidate, manage, and protect resources while maintaining more workable alternatives for transportation and development.[b] Common approaches include mitigation banking, conservation banking, in-lieu-fee mitigation, and ecosystem based mitigation.

Example Measures

Establishing metrics can help agencies understand the extent to which alternative activities are successfully leading to the development of more effective environmental mitigation. The following table provides examples of output and outcome measures that an agency can use to track its progress toward meeting the objective. As was discussed earlier in this guide, for each measure an agency would establish targets based on its needs and priorities. The agency would evaluate results achieved compared to the targets it established for itself.

Output Measures	Data Source(s)/ How to Use
Consistent definitions/understanding of mitigation among transportation and resource agencies	Guidelines, current MOU/MOA
Relevant data layers identified, obtained and used in analysis (and reliability/accuracy is known and documented)	Count/calculate which data layers identified as relevant have been obtained and used as compared to target
Resource agency comments addressed in mitigation planning	Documentation of resource agency comments, how the comments were addressed, who was involved, and when/how consultation occurred among agencies
Number/percentage of resource agencies satisfied with mitigation planning process	Stakeholder surveys
Percent of proposed projects with identified environmental constraints and/or mitigation needs	Long-range transportation plan, TIP, Statewide Transportation Improvement Program (STIP), corridor plan
Percent of projects requiring mitigation that are able to be grouped together for multi-project mitigation	Transportation plans, agencies that regulate mitigation banks
Information on potential environmental constraints and opportunities, identified in planning, is provided to project	Staff surveys

---

[a] *Eco-Logical: An Ecosystem Approach to Developing Infrastructure Projects* http://www.environment.fhwa.dot.gov/ecological/eco_4.asp.
[b] FHWA Policy Memo: Guidelines for Federal-aid Participation in the Establishment and Support of Wetland Mitigation Banks http://www.fhwa.dot.gov/legsregs/directives/policy/memo55.htm.

Output Measures	Data Source(s)/ How to Use
implementing agencies, including an explanation of the analyses and decisions	
Number of projects that can feed into regional mitigation plans	Regional mitigation plans; GIS data

Outcome Measures	Data Source(s)/ How to Use
High priority environmental habitats and connections between them are protected	Use indicators from GIS data and discussions with resource experts at appropriate agencies such as: • acres of land preserved; • number or type of species protected, and • number of projects that protect critical habitat.[31]

Examples in Practice

[31] As part of Maryland DOT's objective to preserve and enhance the State's natural, community, and historic resources, the Maryland Port Administration measures the acres of wetlands or wildlife habitat created, restored, or improved since the year 2000.

Sample Objective 4

Utilize planning level information and products in NEPA analysis and documentation.

Purpose

The transportation planning process and the environmental analysis conducted during project development should work in tandem, with the results of the transportation planning process informing the NEPA process. In practice, however, the analyses used to prepare transportation plans are sometimes disconnected from the analyses performed in NEPA. In addition, there is often no overlap in personnel between the planning and NEPA stages of a project. As a result, the work performed in planning is often duplicated during project development, leading to delays, public confusion, and an inefficient use of resources.

Current law encourages the integration of the information, products and decisions developed during transportation planning into the NEPA process (see 23 CFR 450 and 318), including informing the Purpose and Need Statement; scoping and alternatives identification, evaluation and/or elimination of alternatives, and indirect and cumulative impacts assessment.[c] In order for the analyses or decisions from the planning process to be used in the NEPA process, they must meet certain standards established by NEPA. The successful integration of transportation planning requires that, at a minimum, transportation agencies engage specific stakeholders, including Federal, Tribal, State, and local environmental, regulatory, and resource agencies as well as the public, in the transportation planning process to ensure that the appropriate environmental information is considered.

In addition, planning decisions must be documented in a format that can easily be appended to the NEPA document or incorporated by reference. The information should be thorough and include the reasons behind those decisions, so that the information can be understood by NEPA practitioners who were not involved in planning analyses and decisions. It is important that transportation planning information, analyses, documents, and decisions be well documented and be provided for examination during the scoping process, so that they will have standing in the NEPA process and its additional analyses.

By linking planning and NEPA, transportation agencies can create one cohesive flow of information, resulting in greater predictability and tighter timeframes in project delivery. However, integrating the two processes can be challenging, particularly when the agency conducting the planning differs from the agency developing the NEPA analysis.

Tips for Developing Strategies and Setting Targets

When developing strategies to utilize planning level information within the NEPA process, transportation agencies should:

Identify the appropriate stakeholders to engage during planning – Environmental resource and regulatory agencies, tribal governments and the public must be engaged during the transportation planning process to ensure that the appropriate environmental information is considered in planning. This

---

[c] The Montana Business Process to Link Planning Studies and NEPA/Montana Environmental Policy Act (MEPA) Reviews defines how Montana DOT develops the Purpose and Need Statement, preliminary identification, and review of alternatives during the corridor planning process. For more information, see http://www.mdt.mt.gov/publications/docs/brochures/corridor_study_process.pdf.

can lead to information prepared in such a way that it can be applied in NEPA. As highlighted in Objective 1, it is important that when engaging such stakeholders, the transportation agency should be up front about its intent to use planning level information as the foundation for when the project development/NEPA process begins.

Consider how such agencies will be involved in the following aspects of planning:

- Development of regional transportation vision and policy goals,
- Identification of individual project's Purpose and Need,
- Identification of environmental issues to be evaluated at the planning stage, and
- Development and elimination of alternatives during the planning process.

Consider conducting corridor and subarea studies – A corridor or subarea study can be developed during the planning process to assess considerations on project need, feasibility, and potential resource impacts. If well documented, and with the involvement of resource agencies and the public, analyses and decisions can then be used in scoping during the NEPA process. Agencies should consider:

- Developing criteria for when to develop corridor plans so the data and analyses will be timely and relevant, and
- Developing guidelines to incorporate social, economic, and environmental considerations in the study process, including a process on how to engage appropriate stakeholders.

Consider organizational structure – Consider how the planning and environmental units within the State DOT are organized. For MPOs, if the planning and environmental units do not exist within the agency, consider how the planning and NEPA nexus will be established. Creating a stronger linkage between the two departments is essential for successful integration of planning and NEPA. Because MPO long-range planning is typically removed from the NEPA process, it is particularly important for MPO and State DOT staffs to establish communication and develop information sharing protocols. To improve coordination, agencies can consider convening interdisciplinary teams to share expertise or offering cross-training opportunities, such as planning for non-planners and NEPA training for planning staff.

Develop standard documentation criteria – Consider developing standard documentation criteria so that staff members understand the level of detail required to utilize planning decisions in NEPA. Since the transportation planners will be developing a product that NEPA practitioners will rely on, it is imperative that both planners and NEPA practitioners work together to develop the documentation standards. Planners and practitioners should consider the following when developing standards:

- What information, and level of detail, do NEPA practitioners need to be confident that what they receive is valid and useful in NEPA?[d]
- What format does the information need to be in so that it can be shared during the NEPA scoping process and used as supporting documentation in NEPA?

Example Measures

Establishing metrics can help agencies understand the extent to which their activities successfully link planning information to be used in NEPA. The following table provides examples of output and outcome measures that an agency can use to track its progress toward meeting the objective, as well as possible

---

[d] The Colorado DOT and FHWA Colorado Division Office developed a PEL Questionnaire to help planning and environmental staff document and link corridor planning studies with the NEPA process. For more information, see http://www.environment.fhwa.dot.gov/integ/case_colorado2_quest.asp.

data sources for the measures. As was discussed earlier in this guide, for each measure an agency would establish targets based on its needs and priorities. The agency would evaluate results achieved compared to the target it established for itself.

Output Measures	Data Source(s)/ How to Use
Presence of clearly defined criteria to document planning decisions for use in NEPA	Guidance and/or templates developed
Relevant resource and/or regulatory agencies participating in planning activities	Track attendance at meetings to identify the agencies participating as compared to the target number.
Corridor planning studies developed	Track number of plans developed that have been used to assist in the NEPA decision making process
Percentage of planning staff attending NEPA trainings; percentage of NEPA staff attending planning training	Track attendance at trainings of individuals who are actually involved in the decision-making process or will have continued participation in the process
Same relevant data used in both planning and project development	Documentation of data layers used in analysis as compared to the target number/percentage
Contracts for scoping and project development include review of planning documents	Review contract language

Outcome Measures	Data Source(s)/ How to Use
Decrease in the number of major design changes due to environmental factors in project development	Track the number and reason for major design changes
Decrease in number of permit modifications	Track the number and reason for permit modifications
Decrease in cost/time of developing NEPA document	Track cost and timeliness of developing the NEPA document and compare to average historical costs and timeframes
Decreased time spent revisiting planning decisions in NEPA (for projects with a relevant planning study)	Length of time to complete NEPA review (from a specific start such as programming or development of the Purpose & Need to a specific end point, such as the Record of Decision)
Decreased project costs (for projects with a relevant planning study)	Percent of estimated project cost as compared to final project cost[41]
Decreased time to develop projects (for projects with a relevant planning study)	Average number of years from the programmed commitment in the STIP to construction completion[42]

Examples in Practice

[41] The MoDOT tracks the percent of projects completed within the programmed amount. The completed costs include design, ROW purchases, utilities, construction, inspection, and other miscellaneous costs. These can be compared to the original programmed amounts to determine whether streamlining efforts lead to reductions in project costs.

[42] MassHighway measures its success in delivering STIP projects on schedule by the percentage of projects that begin the construction contract phase in the same year they were programmed. MassHighway also measures actual project completion dates compared to scheduled completion dates, and tracks the causes of construction time extensions. The schedule comparisons can help to determine whether streamlining efforts lead to reductions in project delays.

Conclusions

This guide is intended to serve as a resource for transportation agencies interested in measuring their successes in integrating transportation planning and environmental analysis. While it provides many example measures for use in integration efforts, the list is by no means exhaustive. Agencies beginning measurement programs should remember the following key points:

- **Focus on the measures most relevant to your situation and needs.** It can be tempting to develop measures based on the type of data readily available. It is more appropriate and meaningful, however, to first identify the measures that will be of the most use to your agency, and then determine how to obtain the data if it is not readily available. When beginning a measurement program, focus on the critical few measures that will help you determine if the policy and investment decisions are yielding the desired results.

- **Use different types of measures.** A successful program will include a combination of output and outcome, as well as quantitative and qualitative measures to tell a well-rounded story.

- **Use versatile data sources.** Often, one data source can provide information to serve multiple measures. For example, a stakeholder survey can be designed to collect data to address a variety of topics related to integrated planning, environmental stewardship, data sharing, and coordination. Also, data collected for other performance measuring within the agency may be relevant to measuring success in integrating transportation planning and environmental analysis.

- **Use versatile measures.** Just as one data source can provide information to serve multiple measures, one measure may be able to measure success toward multiple objectives. Several of the measures listed in this guide are relevant to more than one objective, as shown in the summary tables of measures in Appendix A.

APPENDIX A: Summary of Measures

Table 1: Summary of Output Measures

Output Measure	Objective				Data Source
	1	2	3	4	
Number of cross-agency trainings conducted	X			X	Track trainings offered
Number of staff/agencies that participate in training (managers and professionals)	X			X	Track attendance at staff trainings of individuals who are actually involved in the decision-making process or will have continued participation in the process
Number of natural, cultural, and historic resource agencies at the Federal, Tribal, State, regional, and local level involved in an interagency committee	X				Execution of agency agreements
Number of interagency meetings conducted	X				Track number of meetings
Participation rate of members in interagency meetings that focus on input to transportation plans	X				Track attendance at interagency meetings of individuals who are actually involved in the decision-making process or will have continued participation in the process
Number of resource and/or regulatory agencies that have positions dedicated to ensuring coordination with transportation planning	X				Track funding provided to agencies to support transportation planning activities
Agency has clearly articulated and published environmental policy and/or conservation strategies from which to base future decisions		X			Compare policy and/or strategies with current implementation practices
Relevant data layers identified, obtained and used in analysis (and reliability/accuracy is known and documented)		X	X		Count/calculate which data layers identified as relevant have been obtained and used as compared to the target.
Relevant environmentally-sensitive areas identified and mapped		X			Count the number/percent of environmentally-sensitive areas that have been mapped as compared to the target
Transportation network miles with up-to-date resource maps		X			Identify the percentage of available resource mapping and compare to transportation network
Social/economic/environmental criteria used in project selection and prioritization		X			Presence of criteria, which is used in decisionmaking
Proposed projects achieving a target score on the environmental/priority screening		X			Tally scores of evaluated projects to identify which projects meet the target score
Projects that either avoid or minimize impacts		X			Identify project activity in the vicinity of a known threatened or endangered species or critical

Output Measure	Objective				Data Source
	1	2	3	4	
					habitat
Consistent definitions/understanding of mitigation among transportation and resource agencies			X		Guidelines, current MOU/MOA
Resource agency comments addressed in mitigation planning			X		Documentation of resource agency comments, how the comments were addressed, who was involved, and when/how consultation occurred among agencies
Number/percentage of resource agencies satisfied with mitigation planning process			X		Stakeholder surveys
Percent of proposed projects with identified environmental constraints and/or mitigation needs			X		Long-range transportation plan, TIP, STIP, corridor plan
Percent of projects requiring mitigation that are able to be grouped together for multi-project mitigation			X		Transportation plans, agencies that regulate mitigation banks
Information on potential environmental constraints and opportunities, identified in planning, is provided to project implementing agencies, including an explanation of the analyses and decisions			X		Staff surveys
Number of projects that can feed into regional mitigation plans			X		Regional mitigation plans; GIS data
Presence of clearly defined criteria to document planning decisions for use in NEPA				X	Guidance and/or templates developed
Relevant resource and/or regulatory agencies participating in planning activities				X	Track attendance at meetings to identify the agencies participating as compared to the target number.
Same relevant data layers used in both planning and project development				X	Documentation of data layers used in analysis
Corridor planning studies developed				X	Track number of plans developed that have been used to assist in the NEPA decision making process
Contracts for scoping and project development include review of planning documents				X	Review contract language

Table 2: Summary of Outcome Measures

Outcome Measure	Objective 1	Objective 2	Objective 3	Objective 4	Data Source
Decrease in the number of major design changes due to environmental factors in project development	X			X	Track the number and reason for major design changes
Satisfaction of resource and regulatory agencies with the transportation planning process	X				Stakeholder surveys
Increase in percentage of stakeholders who felt their input was considered in the development of transportation plans	X				Stakeholder surveys
Decrease in the number of permit modifications	X				Track the number and reason for permit modifications
Regulatory and resource agencies demonstrate a greater understanding of the planning processes and products of transportation agencies (and vice versa)	X				Stakeholder surveys
High-priority environmental habitats and connections between them are protected (e.g. acreage of land preserved; number or type of species protected)		X	X		Use indicators from GIS data and discussions with resource experts at appropriate agencies such as: • acres of land preserved; • number or type of species protected, and • number of projects that protect critical habitat.
Improvement to species, habitats, and wetlands		X			Use indicators such as: • acres of habitat restored versus acres of habitat impacted • acres of wetlands restored • acres of land preserved based on final recommended network versus other alternatives
Decrease in the number of major design changes due to environmental factors in project development				X	Track the number and reason for major design changes
Decrease in number of permit modifications				X	Track the number and reason for permit modifications
Decrease in cost/time of developing NEPA document				X	Track cost and timeliness of developing the NEPA document and compare to average historical costs and timeframes
Decreased time spent revisiting planning decisions in NEPA (for projects with a relevant planning study)				X	Length of time to complete NEPA review (from a specific start such as programming or development of the Purpose & Need to a specific end point, such as the Record of Decision)
Decreased project costs (for projects with a relevant planning study)				X	Percent of estimated project cost as compared to final project cost
Decreased time to develop projects (for projects with a relevant planning study)				X	Average number of years from the programmed commitment in the STIP to construction completion

APPENDIX B: References

Examples in Practice

Collaborative Environmental and Transportation Agreement for Streamlining (2008). *Progress Report and Approved Work Plan.* Available at ftp://ftp.odot.state.or.us/techserv/Geo-Environmental/Environmental/Other%20Enviromental%20Materials/CETAS/Annual%20Reports%20and%20Work%20Plans/2008_2010_Workplan/CETAS_2008-2010_Work_Plan_AdoptedFinal.pdf

Florida Department of Transportation (2008). *Efficient Transportation Decision Making Performance Management Program: Practitioner's Guide.*

Maryland Department of Transportation. *2009 Annual Attainment Report on Transportation System Performance.* Available at http://www.mdot.state.md.us/Planning/Plans%20Programs%20Reports/Reports/Attainment%20Reports/2009_Attainment_Report.pdf

Massachusetts Highway Department (2009). Scorecard 2009. Available at http://www.mhd.state.ma.us/downloads/ScoreCard/ScoreCard0609.pdf

Missouri Department of Transportation, (2009). *TRACKER.* Available at http://www.modot.mo.gov/about/documents/Tracker_PDF_July09/July09Tracker.pdf

New York State Department of Transportation, (2009). *GreenLITES: Recognizing Leadership In Transportation and Environmental Sustainability.* Available at https://www.nysdot.gov/programs/greenlites/.

Venner Consulting and Parsons Brinkerhoff, (2004). *Environmental Stewardship Practices, Procedures, and Policies for Highway Construction and Maintenance,* National Cooperative Highway Research Program Project 25-25(4), Washington, D.C.

Virginia Department of Transportation, (2006). *Virginia's Transportation Performance Report.* Available at http://www.virginiadot.org/projects/vtrans/VDOT%20final_reduced.pdf

Literature

Alliance for Transportation Research Institute (June 2006). *Context Sensitive Solutions Performance Measures Literature Review.* New Mexico DOT. Available at http://knowledge.fhwa.dot.gov/cops/pm.nsf/All+Documents/F16143C4848E55CB8525737D005D3205/$File/CSS.pdf

Barolsky, R. (2005). *Performance Measures to Improve Transportation Planning Practice.* Transportation Research Circular E-C073. Available at http://onlinepubs.trb.org/Onlinepubs/circulars/ec073.pdf

Cambridge Systematics (2008). *NCHRP 25-25, Task 23: Guidelines for Environmental Performance Measurements Final Report.* Washington, D.C.: Transportation Research Board; Cambridge Systematics, Incorporated. Available at http://www.trb.org/NotesDocs/25-25(23)_FR.pdf

Cambridge Systematics. (2000). *NCHRP Report 446: A Guidebook for Performance-Based Transportation Planning.* Washington, D.C.: Transportation Research Board; Cambridge Systematics, Incorporated. Available at http://onlinepubs.trb.org/onlinepubs/nchrp/nchrp_rpt_446.pdf

Distillate (2008). *Advice on selecting indicators for sustainable transport.* Available at http://www.distillate.ac.uk/outputs/C2%20Selecting%20Indicators%20Report%20(09-04-08).pdf

Gallup Organization. (2007). *Final Report: Implementing Performance Measurement in Environmental Streamlining.* Washington, D.C.: U.S. Department of Transportation; Gallup Organization. Available at http://www.environment.fhwa.dot.gov/strmlng/gallup_05-07.asp

Hendren and Meyers (2006). *NCHRP Project 08-36, Task 53 (02): Peer Exchange Series on State and Metropolitan Transportation Planning Issues. Meeting 2: Non-Traditional Performance Measures.* Transportation Research Board, Washington, D.C. Available at http://www.transportation.org/sites/planning/docs/NCHRP%208-36(53)(2)%20NonTraditional%20Perf%20Measures.pdf

Meyer, M. (2001). *Measuring That Which Cannot Be Measured - At Least According to Conventional Wisdom.* Report of a Conference, Irvine, California, October 29 - November 1, 2000. Performance Measures to Improve Transportation Systems and Agency Operations, pp 105-125. Available at http://www.trb.org/publications/conf/reports/cp_26.pdf

Office of Management and Budget (2003). *Performance Measurement Challenges and Strategies.* Available at http://www.whitehouse.gov/omb/part/challenges_strategies.html

Poister, T. H. (2005). Performance Measurement in Transportation: State of the Practice. *Second National Conference on Performance Measures (*36) pp 81-98. Available at http://onlinepubs.trb.org/onlinepubs/conf/CP36.pdf

Wisconsin Department of Transportation (2007). *State DOT Environmental Programs: Evaluation and Performance Measures Research, Development, and Technology Transfer.* Madison, Wisconsin. Available at http://on.dot.wi.gov/wisdotresearch/database/tsrs/tsrdotenvironmentalprograms.pdf

TransTech Management, Inc. (2004). *NCHRP Web Document 69: Performance Measures for Context Sensitive Solutions - A Guidebook for State DOTs.* Washington, D.C.: National Cooperative Highway Research Program. July, 15, 2007, Available at http://trb.org/publications/nchrp/nchrp_w69.pdf

Vanesse Hangen Brustlin, Inc. (2005 November). *NCHRP 79: Monitoring, Analyzing, and Reporting on Environmental Streamlining Pilot Projects.* Washington, D.C.: Transportation Research Board. Available at http://onlinepubs.trb.org/Onlinepubs/nchrp/nchrp_w79.pdf

Venner, M. (2005). *NCHRP Project 25-25, Task 10: Early Mitigation for Net Environmental Benefit: Meaningful Off-Setting Measures for Unavoidable Impacts.* Transportation Research Board, Washington, D.C. Available at http://www.trb.org/NotesDocs/25-25(10)_FR.pdf

Washington Department of Transportation. *Performance Measurement Criteria Checklist.* Available at http://www.co.washington.or.us/DEPTMTS/auditor/performance/doing_pm/evaluating_pm/checklist_evaluating_pm.pdf

www.ingramcontent.com/pod-product-compliance
Lightning Source LLC
Chambersburg PA
CBHW080937290526
45795CB00007BA/2793